Eat to Beat Kidney Disease

The Only Recipe Book You Will Ever Need to Maintain Healthy Kidneys

BY

Rachael Rayner

License Notes

No part of this Book can be reproduced in any form or by any means including print, electronic, scanning or photocopying unless prior permission is granted by the author.

All ideas, suggestions and guidelines mentioned here are written for informative purposes. While the author has taken every possible step to ensure accuracy, all readers are advised to follow information at their own risk. The author cannot be held responsible for personal and/or commercial damages in case of misinterpreting and misunderstanding any part of this Book

Table of Contents

Introduction

According to the National Kidney Foundation, almost 26 million American adults suffer from chronic kidney disease. There are millions more who are at high risk or have symptoms that they are no aware of. Opinions are divided as to whether the condition is reversable, but I can only speak from personal experience. My own husband was diagnosed with chronic kidney disease in June 2017, due to the high medical expenses, he was unable to afford the dialysis treatment he required. I was not willing to give up on my husband, and it was at this point that I decided to do some research into the condition and found that it can be cured by changing your diet. I am pleased to say that today my husband is kidney disease free!

The doctors couldn't understand what had happened and refused to accept that it was down to a change in diet, but we know otherwise! During my research, I found some really interesting facts about the condition; here are some of them:

- Approximately 13 percent of adults in the United States suffer from chronic kidney disease.
- The leading causes of chronic kidney disease are high blood pressure and diabetes.
- Although we are born with two kidneys, we only need one for the body to function.
- Native Americans, Hispanics, and African Americans are more likely to develop chronic kidney disease than Caucasians.
- There are over 90,000 patients in the United States waiting for a kidney transplant but every year, only 18,000 will get a transplant.

Foods Not to Eat When You've Got Kidney Disease

Some of the foods on this list are not going to make any sense because they are things we are told to eat to stay healthy. However, one of the main dietary requirements for those with kidney disease is to reduce your sodium, phosphorous and potassium intake, and many healthy foods are high in these nutrients. You can go back to them once your kidneys are back to full health, but until then, it is better that you avoid them.

It is also significant to note that you will find some of these foods in the recipe ingredients, but they are the low nutrient version; in other words, if you can't find the low nutrient version – don't eat them.

- Chips, pretzels and crackers
- Prunes, raisins and dates
- Beet greens, spinach and Swiss Chard
- Pre-made, packaged and instant meals
- Sweet potatoes, potatoes
- Apricots
- Processed meats
- Relish, olives, pickles
- Orange juice and oranges
- Dairy
- Bananas
- Brown rice
- Whole wheat bread
- Canned foods

- Avocados
- Dark colored soda

Foods to Eat with Kidney Disease

Foods that are high in antioxidants help protect the body by neutralizing free radicals. Many of these foods make excellent choices for people suffering from chronic kidney disease or dialysis patients. Eating healthy foods and sticking to a renal friendly diet is important for people with kidney disease because they have high levels of inflammation in the body and are at greater risk of cardiovascular disease. Here are some of the healthy foods that are going to be of most benefit to you:

- Olive oil
- Fish
- Egg whites
- Red grapes
- Cranberries
- Strawberries
- Raspberries
- Blueberries
- Onions
- Apples
- Cherries
- Garlic
- Red bell peppers
- Cauliflower
- Cabbage

Get one step closer to full kidney health by stocking up your pantry with this delicious range of kidney friendly foods that you can continue to consume even after the health of your kidney's has been restored.

Breakfast Recipes

Hot Mixed Grain Cereal

Cooking Time: 35 Minutes/**Serves:** 4 Servings

Protein: 4 grams/Sodium:33 milligrams/Potassium:116 milligrams/Phosphorus: 130 milligrams/Carbohydrates: 34 grams/Fat: 1 gram/Calories: 159

A delicious combination of grains and fruit to start your day!

Ingredients

- ½ teaspoon of ground cinnamon
- 6 tablespoons of couscous, plain and uncooked
- 1 cup of apple, sliced and peeled
- 2 tablespoons of buckwheat, uncooked
- 2 tablespoons of bulgur, uncooked
- ¼ cup of rice milk, vanilla
- 2 ¼ cups of water

Directions

1. Heat the milk and water over medium-high heat in a medium-sized saucepan and let the ingredients boil.

2. Add the buckwheat, bulgur and apple.

3. Turn the heat down to low and leave the ingredients to simmer, stir occasionally until the bulgur becomes tender. This should take around 25 minutes.

4. Take the saucepan off the cooker, add the cinnamon and the couscous and stir to combine.

5. Put the lid onto the saucepan and leave it to rest of 10 minutes before fluffing with a fork.

6. Divide into bowls and serve

Egg in the Hole

Cooking Time: 10 Minutes/**Serves:** 2 Servings

Protein: 109 milligrams/Sodium: 204 milligrams/Potassium: 109 milligrams/Phosphorus: 119 milligrams/Carbohydrates: 12 grams/Fat: 29 grams/Calories: 304

There is so much more you can do with your eggs than fry or scramble them!

Ingredients

- Freshly ground black pepper
- A pinch of cayenne pepper
- 2 tablespoons of fresh, chopped chives
- 2 eggs
- ¼ cup of unsalted butter
- 2 slices of Italian bread, ½ an inch thick

Directions

1. Use a small glass or a cookie cutter to cut a 2-inch round out of the middle of each piece of bread.

2. Melt the butter over medium temperature in a large non-stick frying pan.

3. Put the bread into the frying pan and toast it for 30 seconds on each side.

4. Break the eggs into the cut-out holes in the middle of the bread and cook for approximately 2 minutes. Make sure the eggs are set and the bread has turned a golden brown in color.

5. Top with the black pepper, cayenne pepper and chives.

6. Repeat with the other slice of bread, arrange onto plates and serve.

Baked Pancake

Cooking Time: 35 Minutes/**Serves:** 2 Servings

Protein: 7 grams/Sodium: 79 milligrams/Potassium: 106 milligrams/Phosphorous: 73 milligrams/Carbohydrates: 30 grams/Fat: 1 gram/Calories: 161

I bet that you never thought you could bake a pancake! You will never want to eat a fried one again after you've tasted this!

Ingredients

- Cooking spray to grease the skillet
- A pinch of ground nutmeg
- 4 teaspoons of ground cinnamon
- ½ cup of all-purpose flour
- ½ cup of rice milk, unsweetened
- 2 eggs

Directions

1. Prepare the oven by heating it to 450 degrees F.

2. Whisk together the rice milk and eggs in a medium-sized bowl.

3. Add the nutmeg, cinnamon and flour and continue to stir until everything is combined but still a bit lumpy.

4. Spray an oven-proof frying pan with cooking spray and heat it in the oven for 5 minutes.

5. Next, pour the batter into the frying pan and put it back into the oven to bake for 20 minutes. The pancake is cooked when its crispy around the edges and puffed up.

6. Remove from the oven, transfer onto plates and serve.

French Toast Stuffed with Strawberries Cream Cheese

Cooking Time: 1 Hour 5 Minutes/**Serves:** 4 Servings

Protein: 9 grams/Sodium: 270 milligrams/Potassium: 105 milligrams/Phosphorous: 102 milligrams/Carbohydrates: 30 grams/Fat: 9 grams/Calories: 233

You are going to want to eat this for breakfast, lunch and dinner!

Ingredients

- ¼ teaspoon of ground cinnamon
- 1 tablespoon of granulated sugar
- 1 teaspoon of pure vanilla extract
- ½ cup of rice milk, unsweetened
- 8 slices of thick white bread
- 4 tablespoons of strawberry jam
- ½ cup of plain cream cheese
- Cooking spray to grease the baking dish

Directions

1. First, spray the baking dish with cooking spray and put it to one side.

2. Combine the jam and cheese in a small bowl and mix together thoroughly.

3. Spread 3 tablespoons of the cream mixture over 4 slices of bread and put the other 4 slices of bread over the top to make sandwiches.

4. Whisk the vanilla, eggs and milk together in a small bowl until the ingredients become smooth.

5. Dip the sandwiches into the egg mixture and arrange them into the baking dish.

6. Pour the rest of the egg mixture on top of the sandwiches and sprinkle cinnamon and sugar over the top.

7. Place foil over the baking dish and leave them it in the fridge overnight.

8. The next day, prepare the oven by heating it to 350 degrees F.

9. Remove the baking tray from the fridge and bake the French toast for 1 hour.

10. Take the foil off the baking tray and bake until the toast turns into a golden brown color. This should take about five minutes.

11. Once cooked, remove from the oven, arrange onto plates and serve.

Scrambled Cheesy Eggs with Fresh Herbs

Cooking Time: 25 Minutes/**Serves:** 4 Servings

Protein: 12 grams/Sodium: 99 milligrams/Potassium: 194 milligrams/Phosphorus: 67 milligrams/Carbohydrates: 2 grams/Fat: 3 grams/Calories: 77 grams

A healthy dose of cheese and eggs to kick start your day!

Ingredients

- Freshly ground black pepper
- 2 tablespoons of unsalted butter
- 1 tablespoon of fresh tarragon
- 1 tablespoon of finely chopped scallion – the green part only
- ¼ cup of rice milk, unsweetened
- ½ cup of cream cheese, room temperature
- 2 egg whites, room temperature
- 3 eggs, room temperature

Directions

1. Combine the tarragon, scallions, rice milk, cream cheese, egg whites and eggs in a medium bowl and whisk together thoroughly.

2. Heat the butter in your large frying pan over medium-high heat.

3. Add the egg mixture and stir until it turns into a scramble. Season with salt and pepper.

4. Divide onto plates and serve.

Pineapple and Blueberry Smoothie

Cooking Time: 15 Minutes/**Serves:** 2 Servings

Protein: 1 gram/Sodium: 3 milligrams/Potassium: 192 milligrams/Phosphorous: 28 milligrams/Carbohydrates: 22 grams/Fat: 1 gram/Calories: 87

There are no words to describe how rich, creamy, smooth and delicious this is!

Ingredients

- ½ cup of water
- ½ apple
- ½ cup of English cucumber
- ½ cup of pineapple chunks
- 1 cup of frozen blueberries

Directions

1. Combine all the ingredients into a food processor and blend until smooth.

2. Pour into glasses and serve.

Chai-Apple Smoothie

Serves: 2 Servings/**Cooking Time:** 40 Minutes

Protein: 1 grams/Sodium 47 milligrams/Potassium: 92 milligrams/Phosphorous: 74 milligram/Carbohydrates: 1 gram/Calories: 88

Kick start your day with this energy-infused smoothie!

Ingredients

- 2 cups of ice
- 1 apple, peeled, chopped and cored
- 1 chai tea bag
- 1 cup of rice milk, unsweetened

Directions

1. Heat the rice milk in a medium saucepan over a low temperature. Heat until the milk starts to steam, this should take about 5 minutes.

2. Take the milk off the cooker, add the tea bag and leave it to steep and cool down in the fridge for 30 minutes. Take the tea bag out and gently squeeze it to release the flavor.

3. Put the ice, apple and milk into a food processor and blend until smooth.

4. Pour into glasses and serve.

Cheese and Fruit Breakfast Wrap

Cooking Time: 10 Minutes/**Serves:** 2 Servings

Protein: 4 grams/Sodium 177 milligrams/Potassium: 136 milligrams/Phosphorous: 73 milligram/Carbohydrates: 33 grams/Calories: 188

Cheese and fruit make the most delightful combination!

Ingredients

- 1 tablespoon of honey
- 1 apple, peeled, chopped and cored
- 2 tablespoons of plain cream cheese
- 2 flour tortillas, 6 inches

Directions

1. Clean your work surface, lay the tortillas on it and spread one tablespoon of

2. cream cheese over each tortilla leaving around half an inch around the edges.

3. Spread the apple slices in the middle of the tortillas.

4. Drizzle honey over the top, tightly roll up the tortillas and serve.

Egg Curry Pitta Pockets

Cooking Time: 20 Minutes/**Serves:** 4 Servings

Protein: 6 grams/Sodium 134 milligrams/Potassium: 121 milligrams/Phosphorous: 65 milligrams/Carbohydrates: 11 grams/Calories: 178

Get super creative with your eggs and turn them into these delicious pitta pockets!

Ingredients

- 1 cup of roughly chopped watercress
- ½ cup of English cucumber, julienned
- 2 plain pita bread pockets, sliced in half
- 2 tablespoons of light sour cream
- ½ teaspoon of ground ginger
- 1 teaspoon of curry
- 2 teaspoons of unsalted butter
- ½ finely chopped red bell pepper
- 1 finely chopped scallion
- 3 beaten eggs

Directions

1. In a small bowl combine the scallion, red pepper and eggs and whisk together thoroughly.

2. In a large non-stick frying pan, melt the butter over a medium temperature.

3. Pour the egg mixture into the frying pan and cook until the eggs are set, this should take about 3 minutes. Remove the frying pan from the cooker. Then, set it to one side.

4. Next, in a small bowl, combine the sour cream, ginger and curry powder. Whisk together thoroughly.

5. Spread the curry sauce over the pita bread halves.

6. Evenly divide the watercress and the cucumber between the halves.

7. Spoon the eggs into the halves and serve.

Veggie and Egg Muffin

Cooking Time: 35 Minutes/**Serves:** 4 Servings

Protein: 7 grams/Sodium: 75 milligrams/Potassium: 117 milligrams/Phosphorous: 110 milligrams/Carbohydrates: 3 grams/Calories: 84

Make the most of your left-over vegetables incredibly delicious by adding them to some eggs!

Ingredients

- Cooking spray
- 4 eggs
- 2 tablespoons of rice milk, unsweetened
- ½ finely chopped sweet onion
- ½ finely chopped red bell pepper
- 1 tablespoon of fresh parsley, chopped
- A pinch of red pepper flakes
- A pinch of freshly ground black pepper

Directions

1. Prepare the oven by heating it to 350 degrees F.

2. Spray a muffin pan with cooking spray and set it to one side

3. In a large bowl whisk together the onion, milk, eggs, black pepper, red pepper flakes, parsley and red bell pepper and whisk to combine.

4. Pour the egg mixture into the muffin pan.

5. Put the muffin pan in the oven and bake for 20 minutes until the muffins are golden and puffed.

6. Remove the muffins from the oven and serve.

Lunch Recipes

Pepper and Tarragon Pasta Salad

Cooking Time: 45 Minutes/**Serves:** 4 Servings

Protein: 4 grams/Sodium: 2 milligrams/Potassium: 147 milligrams/Phosphorous: 46 milligrams/Carbohydrates: 20 grams/Calories: 156

A delicious meal on its own or a tasty addition to a BBQ!

Ingredients

- 1 tablespoon of dried tarragon
- 2 tablespoons of extra virgin olive oil
- 1 teaspoon of black pepper
- ¼ finely sliced red onion
- ½ finely diced cucumber
- 1 finely sliced red bell pepper
- 2 cups of white pasta

Directions

1. Boil a large saucepan of water and cook the pasta according to the directions on the packet.

2. Once cooked, drain the water from the pasta and leave it to cool down.

3. Add the rest of the ingredients to the pasta and toss to combine.

4. Divide onto plates and serve.

Apple and Brie Salad

Cooking Time: 5 Minutes/**Serves:** 2 Servings

Protein: 4 grams/Sodium: 121 milligrams/Potassium: 120 milligrams/Phosphorous: 48 milligrams/Carbohydrates: 5 grams/Calories: 80

If you enjoy a good old crunch on your salad, you are going to love this!

Ingredients

- ½ peeled apple, cored and diced
- ½ cup of sliced brie
- 1 teaspoon of white wine vinegar
- 1 cup of watercress

Directions

1. Put the watercress into a medium sized bowl and toss with vinegar.

2. Add the apple and brie and toss to combine.

3. Serve with crackers or Melba toast.

Curried Couscous and Baked Salmon

Cooking Time: 25 Minutes/**Serves:** 2 Servings

Protein: 4 grams/Sodium: 176 milligrams/Potassium: 194 milligrams/Phosphorous: 43 milligrams/Carbohydrates: 20 grams/Calories: 220

This meal is light, tasty and ready in less than 30 minutes!

Ingredients

- 1 tablespoon of chili powder
- 1 tablespoon of curry powder
- 2 cups of water
- 1 cup of chicken stock
- 2 cloves of minced garlic
- 1 diced green onion
- 2 tablespoons of extra virgin olive oil
- 2 salmon steaks
- Salt and black pepper
- The juice of 1 lemon

Directions for the Couscous

1. First, heat the olive oil in your large saucepan over a medium temperature.

2. Add the garlic, onions and sauté until they become soft, this should take around 2 minutes.

3. Add the couscous and stir until it becomes slightly toasted.

4. Add the water, the chicken stock, increase the heat to high and once it starts to boil, reduce the heat to low.

5. Add the chili powder and the curry.

6. Put a lid over the saucepan and leave the ingredients to simmer until the couscous has soaked up the majority of the liquid. This should take around 20 minutes.

7. Stir through the couscous with a fork

Directions for the Salmon

1. Heat the oven to 350 degrees F.

2. Line a baking tray with foil.

3. In your small bowl, combine the lemon juice and salt and pepper.

4. Arrange the salmon on the baking tray and brush it with the lemon mixture.

5. Bake the salmon for 20 minutes until it flakes when poked with a fork.

6. Once cooked, remove from the oven and serve with the couscous.

Cauliflower and Onion Curried Soup

Cooking Time: 50 Minutes/**Serves:** 4 Servings

Protein: 4 grams/Sodium: 59 milligrams/Potassium: 400 milligrams/Phosphorous: 94 milligrams/Carbohydrates: 13 grams/Calories: 184

A sumptuous soup bursting with flavours, serves as a starter or a main dish!

Ingredients

- 1 cup of low-fat coconut milk
- 3 cups of water
- 1 cup of chicken broth
- 1 teaspoon of turmeric
- 1 teaspoon of cumin
- 3 sticks of chopped celery
- ½ chopped cauliflower
- 4 cloves of minced garlic
- 1 chopped onion
- 2 tablespoons of coconut oil

Directions

1. In your large saucepan, heat the oil over medium to high heat.

2. Add the cauliflower, garlic and onions leave them to steam for 5 to 10 minutes.

3. Add the spices and celery and cook for a further 5 minutes.

4. Add the water and the stock and once the ingredients start to boil, turn the heat down and simmer until the celery is soft. This should take approximately 15-20 minutes.

5. Take the saucepan from the fire and allow the soup to cool down.

6. Pour the soup into a food processor blend until smooth.

7. Pour the soup back into the saucepan and heat.

8. Add the coconut oil and stir to combine.

9. Sprinkle with black pepper, spoon into bowls and serve.

Pitta Pizza with BBQ Chicken

Cooking Time: 30 Minutes/**Serves:** 2 Servings

Protein: 23 grams/Sodium: 523 milligrams/Potassium: 255 milligrams/Phosphorous: 221 milligrams/Carbohydrates: 37 grams/Calories: 320

Enjoy some tasty BBQ chicken on pitta bread!

Ingredients

- 2 pieces of pita bread
- ⅛ teaspoon of garlic powder
- 4 ounces of cooked chicken
- 2 tablespoons of feta cheese, crumbled
- ¼ cup of purple onion
- 3 tablespoons of barbeque sauce, low sodium
- Cooking spray

Directions

1. Prepare the oven by heating it to 350 degrees F.

2. Grease a baking tray with the cooking spray and arrange the pita bread onto it.

3. Sprinkle the onion over the pitas.

4. Spread the chicken over the top.

5. Sprinkle the feta cheese over the top.

6. Sprinkle the garlic powder over the top.

7. Bake the pitas for 15 minutes.

8. Once cooked, remove from your oven and serve.

Brewery Burger

Cooking Time: 35 Minutes/**Serves:** 4 Servings

Protein: 22 grams/Sodium: 92 milligrams/Potassium: 328 milligrams/Phosphorous: 188 milligrams/Carbohydrates: 7 grams/Calories: 242

Whizz up some ground beef, crackers and eggs for a quick and tasty burger!

Ingredients

- 1 pound of 85% ground beef
- 1 teaspoon of no salt seasoning blend
- 1 large egg
- 5 saltless soda crackers
- 3 tablespoons of rice milk
- 4 whole wheat burger buns
- 1 sliced Dill pickle
- 4 lettuce leaves
- 1 tomato sliced into four
- Dijon mustard

Directions

1. Preheat the grill to 160 degrees F.

1. Put the soda crackers into a bowl and crush them.

2. Add the rice milk to the soda crackers and let the crackers soak.

3. Crack the egg into the cracker mixture and whisk to combine.

4. Add the ground beef to the mixture and stir to combine.

5. Use your hands to form the mixture into patties.

6. Arrange the burgers on the grill and cook for 10 minutes.

7. Arrange the burger buns on plates and top with tomatoes, lettuce, pickles and mustard.

8. Put the burgers on top of the burger buns.

9. Top with the other bun and serve.

Tasty Chicken Wraps

Cooking Time: 20 Minutes/**Serves:** 4 Servings

Protein: 22 grams/Sodium: 462 milligrams/Potassium: 215 milligrams/Phosphorous: 103 milligrams/Carbohydrates: 27 grams/Calories: 260

Healthy and delicious, a wonderful assortment of chicken and vegetables piled onto a soft wrap!

Ingredients

- 8 ounces of canned chicken, low sodium
- 2 whole wheat lavash flatbread
- ½ teaspoon of onion powder
- ¼ cup of mayonnaise
- ½ red bell pepper finely chopped
- 1 finely chopped medium carrot
- 1 finely chopped celery

Directions

1. In your small bowl, combine the onion powder and celery.

2. Place the flatbread onto plates and spread the sauce over it.

3. In another medium sized bowl, combine the celery, carrot and bell pepper and toss to combine.

4. Evenly distribute the chicken and the vegetables on one side of each flatbread.

5. Roll the flatbread and secure them with a toothpick.

6. Cut each wrap at a diagonal angle.

Mouth-Watering Shrimp Quesadilla

Cooking Time: 30 Minutes/**Serves:** 4 Servings

Protein: 20 grams/Sodium: 398 milligrams/Potassium: 276 milligrams/Phosphorous: 243 milligrams/Carbohydrates: 26 grams/Calories: 318

With more flavors than you can handle, this meal is perfect for seafood lovers!

Ingredients

- 2 tablespoons of jalapeno cheddar cheese, shredded
- 4 teaspoons of salsa
- 2 tablespoons of sour cream
- 2 burrito size flour tortillas
- ⅛ teaspoon of cayenne pepper
- ¼ teaspoon of ground cumin
- 4 lemon wedges
- 2 tablespoons of chopped cilantro
- 5 ounces of raw shrimp, divined and shelled

Directions

1. Slice the shrimp into bite-sized pieces.

2. In a zip-lock bag, combine the cayenne pepper, cumin and lemon juice.

3. Add the shrimp pieces to the bag, shake to combine and set it to one side to marinate.

4. Heat a frying pan over medium heat. Then, add the marinated shrimp, leave it to stir fry for 2 minutes or until the shrimp become orange in color.

5. Take the frying pan off the cooker and use a slotted spoon to remove the shrimp.

6. Add the sour cream to the frying pan and stir to combine.

7. Heat a clean frying pan and warm the tortillas for 30 seconds.

8. While the tortilla is in the pan, spoon the shrimp mixture over the top.

9. Spread one tablespoon of cheese over the top.

10. Spread one tablespoon of the marinade and sour cream mixture over the top of the shrimp and fold over the tortilla. Flip over the tortilla and heat the other side.

11. Do the same with the same with the other tortilla.

12. Slice tortillas into four pieces, sprinkle cilantro over the top and serve with a lemon wedge.

Waldorf Turkey Salad

Cooking Time: 30 Minutes/**Serves:** 6 Servings

Protein: 17 grams/Sodium: 128 milligrams/Potassium: 296 milligrams/Phosphorous: 136 milligrams/Carbohydrates: 8 grams/Calories: 200

A low-fat sweet salad is great for a tasty side or main dish!

Ingredients

- 2 tablespoons of apple juice
- ¼ cup of mayonnaise
- ½ cup of chopped onion
- 1 cup of chopped celery
- 3 red apples, medium
- 12 ounces of cooked, unsalted turkey breast

Directions

1. In a medium bowl combine the celery, apple and turkey.

2. Add the apple juice and mayonnaise and stir to combine.

3. Divide onto plates and serve.

Beef Tortilla Rollups

Cooking Time: 20 Minutes/**Serves:** 2 Servings

Protein: 24 grams/Sodium: 279 milligrams/Potassium: 448 milligrams/Phosphorous: 253 milligrams/Carbohydrates: 18 grams/Calories: 258

This super quick meal makes the perfect meal for two!

Ingredients

- 1 teaspoon of herb seasoning blend
- 2 romaine lettuce leaves
- 8 slices of cucumber
- ¼ red sweet bell pepper sliced into strips
- ¼ cup of chopped red onion
- 2 tablespoons of whipped cream

Directions

1. Arrange the tortillas onto plates and spread the cream cheese over them.

2. Layer each tortilla with lettuce, cucumbers, pepper strips, red onion, roast beef and red onion.

3. Sprinkle the herb blend seasoning over the top, roll and serve.

Dinner Recipes

Green Bean Casserole

Cooking Time: 45 Minutes/**Serves:** 9 Servings

Protein: 22 grams/Sodium: 80 milligrams/Potassium: 215 milligrams/Phosphorous: 102 milligrams/Carbohydrates: 11 grams/Calories: 173

A light creamy casserole with a unique and creamy flavour!

Ingredients

- 10 Ritz crackers, unsalted
- 3 tablespoons of unsalted butter
- 2 tablespoons of all-purpose flour
- 1 teaspoon of sugar
- 1 cup of sour cream
- ¾ cup of sharp cheddar cheese finely shredded
- 6 cups of frozen green beans, French style
- Cooking spray

Preparation

1. Prepare the oven by heating it to 350 degrees F.

2. Spray a casserole dish with cooking spray.

3. In a small bowl, crush the crackers and set it to one side.

4. Over medium temperature melt 2 tablespoons of butter in a medium frying pan.

5. Add the flour. Then, stir for one minute.

6. Add the cheddar cheese, sour cream and sugar and stir to combine.

7. Add the green beans and stir to combine.

8. Pour the mixture into the casserole dish.

9. Melt 1 tablespoon of butter in the microwave.

10. Pour the butter over the crushed crackers and then sprinkle them on top of the casserole.

11. Bake until the top becomes golden brown, this should take 30 minutes.

Roasted Cauliflower and Carrot Salad

Cooking Time: 35 Minutes/**Serves:** 8 Servings

Protein: 2 grams/Sodium: 134 milligrams/Potassium: 378 milligrams/Phosphorous: 53 milligrams/Carbohydrates: 13 grams/Calories: 160

Sample this warm salad featuring carrot and roasted cauliflower - it's simply delicious!

Ingredients

- ½ cup of pomegranate seeds
- 6 cups of baby leaf lettuce
- ¼ teaspoon of black pepper
- ¼ teaspoon of salt (optional)
- ¼ teaspoon of yellow mustard
- 1 ½ tablespoons of maple syrup
- 3 tablespoons of unseasoned rice vinegar
- 1 tablespoon of Italian seasoning blend
- 6 tablespoons of olive oil
- 1 medium diced onion
- 1 large turnip, skin removed and sliced into bite-sized chunks
- 5 medium carrots, peeled and cut into bite-sized chunks
- 1 small head of cauliflower

Directions

1. Prepare the oven by heating it to 425 degrees F.

2. In a large bowl, combine the onions, turnips, carrots, cauliflower, three tablespoons of olive oil, Italian seasoning blend. Toss to combine.

3. Spread the vegetables out onto the baking tray and put them in the onion for 20 minutes.

4. While the vegetables are cooking, start making the dressing by adding the rest of the olive oil, mustard, maple syrup, rice vinegar and salt and pepper into a bowl. Whisk together thoroughly.

5. Remove the tray from your oven, toss the vegetables and bake for a further 15 minutes, make sure the vegetables are tender before removing them from the oven.

6. Arrange the salad in a bowl and toss with the dressing.

7. Arrange the salad onto plates, top with the roasted vegetables, sprinkle the pomegranate seeds over the top and serve straight away.

Potato, Green Beans and Sheet Pan Chicken Dinner

Cooking Time: 45 Minutes/**Serves:** 4 Servings

Protein: 26 grams/Sodium: 310 milligrams/Potassium: 585 milligrams/Phosphorous: 300 milligrams/Carbohydrates: 26 grams/Calories: 360

A delicious chicken dish saturated with flavour, a super healthy way to get your week started!

Ingredients

- 1 tablespoon of Italian dressing dry mix
- 4 tablespoons of unsalted butter
- 10 ounces of frozen green beans
- 16 ounces of chicken, sliced into thin strips
- 3 cups of red potatoes, peeled and chopped
- Cooking spray

Directions

1. Prepare the oven by heating it to 400 degrees F.

2. Boil the potatoes for 10 minutes in a large pan of water.

3. Drain the water from the potatoes, refill the pan and boil again until the potatoes become tender, this should take around 10 minutes.

4. Drain the water from the potatoes and set them to one side.

5. Spray a baking tray with cooking spray and arrange the chicken on one end of the tray.

6. Arrange the green beans next to the chicken.

7. Arrange the potatoes next to the green beans.

8. Melt the butter in the microwave and pour it over the food on the tray.

9. Sprinkle the Italian dressing dry mix over the top and roast for 30 minutes.

10. Once cooked, remove from the oven, divide onto plates and serve.

Vegetables with Roasted Rosemary Chicken

Cooking Time: 45 Minutes/**Serves:** 4 Servings

Protein: 30 grams/Sodium: 73 milligrams/Potassium: 580 milligrams/Phosphorous: 250 milligrams/Carbohydrates: 8 grams/Calories: 215

It doesn't get any better than this simple meal bursting with summer flavour and color!

Ingredients

- 1 tablespoon of dried rosemary
- 4 chicken breasts with the skin and bone
- ½ teaspoon of ground black pepper
- 1 tablespoon of olive oil
- 8 cloves of crushed garlic
- 1 large red onion, chopped
- ½ a medium bell pepper, chopped
- 1 chopped medium carrot
- 2 medium zucchinis sliced into ½ inch thick rounds

Directions

1. First, prepare your oven by heating it to 375 degrees F.

2. In a roasting pan, combine the vegetables, garlic and season with the black pepper.

3. Roast the vegetables for 10 minutes.

4. Pull the skin up on the chicken rub the rosemary and black pepper onto the flesh. Put the skin back and season the chicken with more rosemary and black pepper.

5. Next, take the baking pan out of the oven and arrange the chicken on top of the vegetables and bake for around 35 minutes.

6. Once cooked, remove from the oven and serve.

Garden Vegetables and Pork Chops

Cooking Time: 35 Minutes/**Serves:** 4 Servings

Protein: 25 grams/Sodium: 377 milligrams/Potassium: 720 milligrams/Phosphorous: 280 milligrams/Carbohydrates: 9 grams/Calories: 352

Juicy pork chops with tasty garden vegetables make a wonderfully filling main course!

Ingredients

- 4 pork chops
- ½ cup of yellow onion
- 1 chopped red medium bell pepper
- 1 chopped medium carrot
- 1 chopped yellow medium squash
- 1 cup of chopped eggplant
- 4 sprigs of fresh thyme
- 1 bay leaf
- ½ teaspoon of pepper
- ½ teaspoon of salt
- 2 tablespoons of minced garlic
- 2 tablespoons of chopped fresh basil
- 3 tablespoons of olive oil

Directions

1. In a small bowl, combine the thyme, bay leaf, salt, pepper, garlic, basil and olive oil and whisk to combine.

2. Place the eggplant, squash, carrot, bell pepper and onions in a large bowl.

3. Drizzle half of the contents in the small bowl over the vegetables and toss to combine.

4. Arrange the pork chops in the bowl and toss with the rest of the olive oil mixture. Stir to combine, put a lid over the bowl and leave it in the fridge overnight.

5. The next day, prepare the oven by heating it to 400 degrees F.

6. Remove the bowl from the fridge and place the contents onto a baking tray.

7. Bake for 20 minutes, make sure the pork is tender before you remove it from the oven.

Green Beans and Sheet Pan Salmon

Cooking Time: 30 Minutes/**Serves:** 4 Servings

Protein: 20 grams/Sodium: 187 milligrams/Potassium: 452 milligrams/Phosphorous: 240 milligrams/Carbohydrates: 4 grams/Calories: 350

A satisfying salmon dish with a healthy dose of greens!

Ingredients

- 4 lemon wedges
- 2 teaspoons of olive oil
- 6 tablespoons of mayonnaise
- 2 tablespoons of finely chopped fresh dill
- ½ pound of fresh trimmed green beans
- 4 salmon fillets
- Cooking spray

Directions

1. First, prepare the oven by heating it to 425 degrees F.

2. Coat a baking tray with cooking spray.

3. In a small bowl, combine the mayonnaise and the dill.

4. Coat the salmon over the top of each salmon fillet and arrange them on the baking tray.

5. Coat the green beans with olive oil and arrange them on the baking tray.

6. Place the baking tray into the oven. Then, bake for 20 minutes.

7. Remove from the oven and serve.

Turkey and Noodles

Cooking Time: 35 Minutes/**Serves:** 8 Servings

Protein: 33 grams/Sodium: 188 milligrams/Potassium: 533 milligrams/Phosphorous: 296 milligrams/Carbohydrates: 22 grams/Calories: 273

Noodles and turkey spruced up with Italian seasoning, you can't go wrong with this dish!

Ingredients

- 1 teaspoon of black pepper
- 1 tablespoon of Italian seasoning
- 1 can of diced tomatoes
- ½ cup of diced green pepper
- ½ cup of chopped green onion
- 2 pounds of lean ground turkey
- 1 tablespoon of olive oil
- 2 cups of elbow macaroni

Directions

1. First, cook your macaroni according to the **Directions** on the packet. Drain and put it to one side.

2. In a large frying pan, heat the oil over medium temperature and cook the turkey.

3. Add the tomatoes, green peppers and onions and season with the black pepper and the Italian seasoning. Stir to combine.

4. Add the macaroni and stir to combine.

5. Cover and leave the ingredients to simmer for 5 minutes.

6. Divide onto plates and serve.

Seafood Croquettes

Cooking Time: 30 Minutes/**Serves:** 8 Servings

Protein: 14 grams/Sodium: 337 milligrams/Potassium: 184 milligrams/Phosphorous: 191 milligrams/Carbohydrates: 11 grams/Calories: 189

It doesn't get any better than these seafood croquettes, you will want to eat them for breakfast, lunch and dinner!

Ingredients

- ¼ cup of mayonnaise
- ½ teaspoon of ground mustard
- 2 tablespoons of lemon juice
- Cooking spray
- ½ cup of plain breadcrumbs
- ½ teaspoon of black pepper
- ¼ cup of chopped onion
- 2 egg whites
- 1 can of salmon, water packed

Directions

1. Drain the water out of the canned salmon.

2. In a medium bowl, combine the salmon, egg whites, onion, black pepper, breadcrumbs, lemon juice, mustard and mayonnaise. Stir to combine.

3. Use your hands to form the mixture into patties.

4. Spray a frying pan with cooking oil and heat it.

5. Cook the patties by browning them on both sides.

6. Remove from the pan and serve.

Seafood Supreme

Cooking Time: 45 Minutes/**Serves:** 6 Servings

Protein: 16 grams/Sodium: 445 milligrams/Potassium: 255 milligrams/Phosphorous: 148 milligrams/Carbohydrates: 20 grams/Calories: 220

A mouth-watering melody of seafood with a crispy topping that will have you everyone who tastes it up for a second helping!

Ingredients

- 1 cup of breadcrumbs
- ½ cup of mayonnaise
- ½ teaspoon of black pepper
- ½ cup of frozen peas
- 1 cup of chopped celery
- 2 tablespoons of chopped green onions
- 4 tablespoons of chopped green pepper
- 1 cup of boiled shrimp
- 1 cup of boiled crabmeat
- Cooking spray

Directions

1. First, prepare the oven by heating it to 375 degrees F.

2. Boil the shrimp and crab meat for 10 minutes.

3. Drain the water and add the green pepper, green onions. celery, frozen peas, black pepper, mayonnaise and stir to combine.

4. Grease a casserole dish and transfer the mixture into it.

5. Top with the breadcrumbs. Then, bake for 30 minutes.

6. Once cooked, remove from your oven and serve.

Fish Tacos

Cooking Time: 40 Minutes/**Serves:** 4 Servings

Protein: 21 grams/Sodium: 138 milligrams/Potassium: 335 milligrams/Phosphorous: 181 milligrams/Carbohydrates: 7 grams/Calories: 164

Delightful crispy fish tacos that are simple to make and perfectly delicious!

Ingredients

- ¼ cup of lemon juice
- 1 teaspoon of garlic powder
- 2 teaspoons of dill weed
- ¼ cup of unsalted margarine or butter
- 20 finely crushed unsalted saltine crackers
- 12-16 fish fillets of your choice

Directions

1. Prepare the oven by heating it to 400 degrees F.

2. In a large bowl, combine the dill, garlic and crackers.

3. Melt the margarine or butter.

4. Dip the fish into the butter, into the crumbs and into the butter again.

5. Arrange on a baking tray and bake for 10 minutes until the fish is flaky.

6. Remove from the oven and serve.

Conclusion

As you have read, kidney disease is due to bad dietary habits, most people who have eaten junk food for the majority of their lives are terrified of the word "healthy eating" because they assume they are missing out on something. Well, the only thing you are missing out on by changing your diet is sickness and disease, and I think you can agree with me that's a great thing to miss out on!

The recipes in this book are tasty and delicious, they will give you strength and energy, but most importantly maintain the health of your kidneys!

I wish you all the best on your journey to disease free kidneys!

Author's Afterthoughts

THANK YOU

Thanks ever so much to each of my cherished readers for investing the time to read this book!

I know you could have picked from many other books, but you chose this one. So, a big thanks for downloading this book and reading all the way to the end.

If you enjoyed this book or received value from it, I'd like to ask you for a favor. Please take a few minutes to post an honest and heartfelt review on Amazon.com. Your support does make a difference and helps to benefit other people.

Thanks for your Reviews!

Rachael Rayner

Made in the USA
Middletown, DE
05 June 2024

55368847R00046